"Koraly Dimitriadis is a p[...]
tenderness of a loving hand[...]
– **Tony Birch, bestselling** [...] Chair in
Australian Literature

"*Just Give Me the Pills* is an extraordinary composition – a defiant portrait of untamed domesticity ... brutal honesty that is candid, unashamed and shockingly moving ... a feminist anthem for social justice and self-love ... a riveting and compulsive read."
– **Bronwyn Lovell, Val Vallis Award winner 2017**

"Relentlessly bold, unapologetic, and humorous at all the right times. If one can detect a new wave of Australian poetry on the rise, it's due in no small part to the pioneering efforts of Koraly Dimitriadis."
– **Ruby Hamad, author, *White Tears, Brown Scars***

"With this second collection of poetry, Koraly's writing gets better and better. There is the same punch and passion of her first collection, yet there is also wonderful moments of quiet and regret. In this long form narrative poem cycle, we see the emergence of a soul out of shame, bitterness and terror into defiance, resolution and strength. It's absolutely authentic and absolutely dynamic."
– **Christos Tsiolkas, award-winning author, *The Slap***

"In her candour and her urgency, Koraly captures the painful, the shameful, the messy in all of us. Koraly's voice is unique, impassioned and grunts and shouts and howls and whispers and cajoles and offers on every page of this book. *Just Give Me the Pills* is an odyssey. A female, Greek-Cypriot-Australian odyssey about being, becoming, about motherhood and marriage, about self-hatred and self-love. It is both intensely personal and broadly universal. It is a guide to self-realisation. A call to arms."
– **Emilie Collyer, award-winning playwright and poet**

"Ms Dimitriadis is the voice of an angry Australia. Her anger is for the disaffected, the voiceless and the invisible.
– **Paul Capsis, award-winning performer**

"She dishes the dirt, and she's not afraid of anything. Her writing is coming for you, so you'd better just accept it .... Energetic and irreverent, a must read."
– *Overland Literary Journal*

Also by Koraly Dimitriadis

Love and Fuck Poems

just give me the
Pills

the illustrated edition

KORALY DIMITRIADIS

outside the box

First published in 2018
Reprinted 2023

Outside The Box Press
www.outsidetheboxpress.com

ISBN 978-0-9872777-8-7

ISBN 978-0-9872777-9-4 (ebook)
ISBN 978-0-9872777-4-9 (original edition)

Illustrations by Rosie G

Author photograph by Kaliopi Malamas

Design and typesetting by Ilura Design
www.ilurapress.com

A catalogue record for this
book is available from the
National Library of Australia

A poem is a fragment in time, it is not the poet

For my daughter

Contents

Preface

Wedding Day Photography

The photography was like artwork from the renaissance era. She was not a girl, she was a painting. Photogenic beauty, the light caressed her at all the right angles. There were no cracks in her skin, flawless, precious porcelain doll, hollow, tap her and she might crack, radiant, immortal, fifty-five kilos, arms as thin as the branches her mum would cut from the tree to smack her with, skin powdery-tablet white, a natural wide smile, betrothed to womanhood, and when she walked down the aisle of the church she was so happy her chest and shoulders broke out in a love-red rash, clearly visible to the three hundred guests from underneath her veil, but she did not care for she had done it, she was the happiest, the happiest a daughter could be, her parents, the happiest and proudest she had ever seen them in her life, for she had reached the pinnacle of her life ...

Slice

my belly like bread
caesar style
wait, wait for the cry
then the sigh
awkward bundle
tiny hands, alien toes
bloodied mush
my guts hidden
suffocating bright light
(am I dead?)
passing back the parcel
to the other side
of the sheet
(what have I done?)

This is how my creativity was reborn

Breastfeed

I said I was going to do it and I did it
even though the nurses and the bottle mums said *You
don't have to*
& I had thrush on my nipples & it was like sandpaper
& Dad came over & I was in my bra and undies & he said
'put some clothes on'
& under the feminist guise I yelled at patriarchy in a way
I never have before
I said, 'Dad, if you don't like it, then get out!'
& it was a first for Dad too, he didn't yell back
went outside for a cigarette

But twelve weeks later it was so nice
how you claimed my boobie as your own
I made it to one year, I wanted to keep going
But everyone was asking when I am going to stop
& don't you think she's a bit old for it
& what will people say if they see you

So I stopped

I denied you your food
I did what I was advised
Just like usual

Crying on Couches & beds

The Bike Ride

We took the bikes today
and went. Zapped down
paths, along the
creeks and beyond

You said we should
I knew I should,
but that I shouldn't
bring my music
or a notebook

I slipped the notebook in
when you weren't watching

The sun was pleasant,
the wind caressed
But the creek stank
Seagulls zigged
sparrows zagged

I forgot what birds looked like

I filled all my lost pockets
with air. It hummed out

We were going really fast,
so fast I thought I might
misjudge the path
tumble down the embankment
smashing my skull
poetically beside
graffiti art
and the Broadmeadows* train

But I didn't

Although a hairy wog*
swore at me on
the road and I almost
lost the bike and
myself.
'Sorry,' I mumbled
with my head low

I grunted up those hills
My thighs stung,
sweat rolled down
my back

I showed those
northern suburbs hills
what I was made of

14

Not what *they* thought
I was made of

I fucking showed those hills

I promised myself
I wouldn't write a poem

Astro Boy

You rescued me like Astro Boy
My husband, my hero
Astro Boy soaring high
Transformers meets the eye
Commodore 64
Pacman, gobble gobble
Atari—River Raid
chug, chug, chug, refuel
SEGA
Sonic vs the Professor
High school, homework
No boyfriends allowed
just friends
Tihous!*
Walls!
TV off at sex
No colouring of hair
No sleeping at friends' houses
Did you watch the news?
A girl was stabbed
Clubbing and curfews
Remember a girl was stabbed
No boyfriends allowed
Just husbands
Kissing, lots of kissing ...

Little Dina

Little Dina, remember when we
hung out in your living room,
my sisters, your sisters,
with the parents in the kitchen?

Remember?

We hung out 'cause we had to—
my dad and your dad
been best of mates
since Cyprus days

You were our baby, little Dina

I think it's been fifteen years since we
hung out in that living room
What you been up to, little Dina?
Where you been?
I've been writing my life away

Today's your wedding day, little Dina
Look at you, all grown up
in that big, white dress
The DJ's playing *Ta Rialia**
and you're dancing your *syrto**.

This is *no* Greek wedding
It's Cypriot

Don't cry during your speech, little Dina,
giggle like you used to
Run to the park
don't waltz on the dance floor
Play with your dolls
don't style your hair and makeup

Where are you, little Dina?
Where'd you go?

All the Effort

All the effort it takes
to ask 'what's wrong?'
between commercial breaks

Work hours stretch
in all directions

Rushed short kisses
when it's too late to talk
and your brain is as mushed
as mashed potato

The toilets need cleaning
The schnitzel needs frying
The child needs minding

and all this
while trying to squeeze love
out of the click click click
of laptop keys ...

Baklava

sweet sugary syrup
Mum's baklava
is renowned in the clan
of wog* gatherings
a dish for every disaster
eat! eat! get fat with children
wipe down your benches
and when was the last time
you mopped your floors?
give her a haircut
look at her, she can't see,
you should dust her room
she can't breathe
she needs her mum
pluck your head
out of the clouds
she needs her mum
take some baklava
come on, take some
take another piece
another, take some
take it ...

Mum's baklava, on my bench going mouldy

Crying on Couches and Beds

During your nap time
I cry on couches and beds
Not sure why I do
When I have everything

It is not normal that I cry like this
Until my eyes are puffy and bruised
I am being unappreciative
Many have told me I must stop this abuse

I pick you up from your cot
When it's time to resume my role
You don't understand
I'm glad that you don't

Sometimes it's the bed
Sometimes it's the couch
Sometimes it's a tissue
Sometimes it's a pen

Sometimes it's not during naptime
It could be after a fight
or when something's not right
& I've shut the bedroom door tight

I've told him not to just leave me
Because when I run out of tears
I end up determined to be dead

But why should he come get me?
It's not his fault I'm like this
I really do just want to be dead
But I can't die, I must live for you

Shopping

mummy took me to the shops today / not shopping,
shops / we had a baby chino / ham and cheese sandwich /
ran / ran / stop, mummy yelled, stop / don't like it when
mummy yells / don't raise the eyes, I said / speak low, I
said / don't run away, she said / didn't, I said / be a good
girl / I'm a good girl / mummy held my hand / walked /
mummy put on a top / she put one on me too / in front
of mirrors / walked / but then I saw the wiggles / wiggles,
mummy / ran / ran / stop, mummy yelled /stop / stop /
smack / cried / cry / crying / don't like it when mummy
yells / mummy hugged me / said sorry / not right to hit /
kissed me, kiss kiss / love you, mummy / don't like it when
mummy cries

Orthodox God

I thirst
I thirst for Him
the Orthodox God
He resides in a domed
church of golden jewels
That is where I will flee
to drink his blood-red wine,
feast on his moist bread
That is where I will flee
to tame my restless soul
To the Orthodox God

Scriptures are set in stone,
the olive leaves crisp
sizzling on my chest
Three times I cross to
painted eyes that stare
I chime faster than your bells
as Holy Smoke hovers
above me. I inhale
My Orthodox God

Black cloaked man
at the lectern of guilt

bou ine i neolea mas?
Where is our youth? you ask,
to an unworthy crowd
Holy Man of interpretations
why do you block me
when my soul is parched
beyond forty days?
Why do you feed me truths
that shove me to damnation
while jiggling keys not yours?

Holy Man of business,
the Orthodox God does reside
in your judgmental eyes
Eyes I hide from
On asphalt altars I will beg,
lips cracked, hand trembling
On high altars my knees will scrape
for one sweet drop of
                    His *blood*

The Prayer of Blood

I am praying, for the trick-trick-tickle
down my legs and between my thighs
It seems that ninety-nine percent confident
isn't so confident after all

I don't want it

I've done it

the alien invasion of my uterus
the abnormal stretching of my skin
the loss of my sanity

society neglecting
to look beyond my belly

I am more than my fucking belly

I have done everything in my power to prevent this
but nature has a way of reclaiming its one percent

Soon everything that is me
will flow like milk into my bosom
to feed my baby ...

my baby ...
my baby ...
my baby ...
my baby ...

No!

Selfish mother, selfish, selfish, selfish ...

I'll pray harder today
I'll pray for God to understand
to keep me whole, to keep me sane

to keep me
                    me

oh   yes   it's   come
                                          blood ...

Motherhood Observations

1. She is afraid of the threat of a scream, but she is more afraid of the scream itself. The scream originates from my father, his metal-stained hands, blood-shot eyes, but its roots can be traced back to the villages of Cyprus, where it was okay to use a belt.

2. She already knows how to negotiate and she's three. When she asks for three chocolate biscuits and I say 'no', she asks for two, and when I say 'no' she settles at one. She also offers me the biscuit first, that way it is okay for her to have some after me, and that's difficult because sometimes chocolate makes everything, semi-okay.

3. She is fascinated by her excrement, but I don't want to talk about it. She asked where it comes from, and I told her 'food', and then she asked if she could eat it. I explained that it was 'yucky' and now she holds it in all day, is afraid of the toilet. She wants me to hold her hand when she goes, and her face reddens when she pushes, her eyes searching mine for answers, comfort, hope. I provide these through my eyes.

4. She enjoys coming into the toilet and asking me if I have my period. She does her own inspection. She also offers to bring me a pad if I do, likes to peel off the sticky bits.

5. She marvels at flowers, the colours, pink, red, white—'Look, Mummy!' she exclaims as we drive past the cemetery. 'Look at all the pretty flowers, Mummy!'

6. When I leave the house, she wants to know where I'm going. I don't want to tell her I'm meeting friends because then she wants to come so I lie and say I'm going to school. It's not a complete lie, I have just started a writing course. I did not return to my job as an accountant after I gave birth. But then one day she drove her battery-operated hummer to my feet while I was applying my makeup and announced she wanted to go to school too. She held up an old bag of mine and inside were pencils and some of her drawings. She stepped off the bike and asked if she could put some makeup on too, said she wanted to be like me.

But I don't want her to be like me.

Simple girl

I Put on My Face

I put on my face
driving / cake it on
thick, creamy
fake skin

I put on my face
cracked / icy-blue blood
through fast veins
hissing

I put on my face
cooked / apron strings tight
on neck flesh
boiling

My face goes on at
Pinocchio moons,
Twinkle stars /
tucked in

My face snaps on at
hospitals / when eyes
beg for an
answer

My face trembles off
in a locked place /
hands shake
breathe in space
sit down
take my brow
words roll out
fucking hell
air is still
take a pill
in the dark
dream of blood
tear at skin
all that sin
faster pace
all that waste
dream of death
on my breath
want a taste
gonna waste
oh my God
quick, quick, quick
oh my God
where's my face
quick, she's coming
where's my face

she can't *see* my face /
   lips
   eyes
   hair dead straight
suck it in
that acid taste
pulling cling wrap
on my face
okay, smile:
there's my face
a little harder
   there's
       my
           face

The Search

The search is on
for information
Enough words
to numb the
mania

The search is on
for music. Pounding
tunes to blast
me to bliss
and beyond

The search is on
on facebook and
twitter, to meet
connect, mesh

The search is on
for something
not sure what

or not

The search is on
for you,

yeah *you*
Search for me
between the
lines
and we'll
entangle
our lives
while
searching
for
nothing

Disappear

Poof!
Into smoke

Come hither, my infection
bury me with shovels
I can breathe, through tiny holes,
to stop invasions of my uterus

Come hither, my infection
dance with me to melodies
Let me live inside your guitar
I can breathe, through tiny holes
(in case you're wondering)

In case you're wondering,
words keep me company

Come hither, my infection
take off my ring
slide it over my head
to my neck
I can choke
through *tiny* holes

Come hither, my infection
lead me to secluded hotels
succumbing to desires
while rolling around
and stroking the
naked flesh of norms
to *press,* gotcha, ha!
shove
fluffy white pillow
strangle the monster
(tentacles fighting)
gotcha, you mother fucker!
can't breathe, it can't breathe
(laughing, in case you're wondering)

Wog* Mum

Fuck the mess
I'm not cleaning
What you looking at, Wog Mum?
Yeah, I don't like cleaning
I hate cooking too
I haven't dusted in two years!
Don't look at me like you're dying, Wog Mum
I'm gonna make somethin' of me
I'm not gonna pop 'em out, one after the other
Don't want more kids, Wog Mum
Don't cross yourself and plead to
God to help me, Wog Mum
I like my life
I'm not gonna end up like you,
cleaning and re-cleaning
re-cleaning the cleaning
I'm gonna make somethin' of me
Breathe, Wog Mum, breathe
I like my life
I'm not gonna end up like you,
staring at walls with
the clocks ticking
and *waiting*
wallowing
evaporating

The Sex Therapist

The sex therapist said we look like we love each other
The sex therapist said we are salvageable

I love you, I just don't want to fuck you

'This is a problem we can fix,' she said

'I am horny all the time,' I said

'She masturbates every day,' you said

'And what do you masturbate to?' she asked

'My ex or guys breaking into my house
or cornering me in public toilets
and gang raping me while I'm crying'

'I am a disgusting human being,' I said

The sex therapist said that it's okay
I can just think of whatever I like when we fuck
and then I can come all over you with my imagination

But I never wanted to have sex in the first place
I just wanted him to hold me tight

hide the razors so they were out of sight
encourage me to keep taking my medicine
until I was somehow became whole again

We take the sex therapist's advice to our bedroom
I don't like looking at bodies naked
I don't like you touching my boobs
I don't like your tongue in my mouth
I don't like any kind of oral

It is very procedural our fucking
You lay on your back
I lay on top, you put it inside me
I think of awful disgusting things
Nobody talks because it distracts my story
I come all over your holy cock

Afterwards I want to take pills
Instead, we cuddle on the couch

These therapists know
what they are talking about

I Can't Wait to Take You to Crèche Tomorrow

And then   I'll breathe
'There,' I'll say to your carer,
'fucking take her'

On the way back home,
music will blare through speakers,
and my ears will bleed

I can't wait to take you to crèche tomorrow
and then nobody will f–o–l–l–o–w me
to the couch
the computer
the shower
the toilet
e–v–e–r–y–w–h–e–r–e

There'll be no pointy elbows
on my bursting bladder
and gagging nappies
and touching my things
and wa wa tears
and tantrums
and biscuits

and 'want this'
and screeching
every
moment
I'm not
staring
at you

I can't wait to take you to crèche tomorrow
to stop myself from smashing the toys
you never play with
To stop fretting
that sharp
edge

I can't wait to take you to crèche tomorrow
to have something for me without you

I can't wait to take you to crèche tomorrow
so I don't have to feed you
and play with you
and read to you
and bathe you
and hear you
not sleep during your nap time
while I suffocate on your cry
so I can have one minute

one *fucking* minute
for *me*

I can't wait to take you to crèche tomorrow
to feel like me for a few hours
to be childless for a few hours
and dance for a few hours
and write for a few hours
stare at your toys for a few hours
linger in your room for a few hours
drown in your absence for a few hours

To run to the crèche
pick you up, breathe you in
my beautiful, gorgeous
precious, baby girl

Simple Girl

Why can't I just be a simple girl
appreciate a well-kept house
a mowed lawn, a sizzling bbq?
Be content with mothering,
having two or three or many?
Why can't I stay seated in the chair?
Why do I roam and search?
Why do I moan and lurch?
Why don't I believe? have faith?

Why can't I stay still?

Why do I whine, why do I rhyme
why do I pine for more?

Why don't I fucking just go to bed?

Why do I feel ill, want to retch,
want to vomit and torment?

Why don't I shut the fuck up?

I could have been happy
I could have baked the *best* cakes
brought pretty things for the house

I could have gone clothes shopping
and been excited about it
I could have let you take care of me
love and adore me forever
till the stars descended on us

This, I could have done
and loved every minute of it

if only, I was a simple girl

The Little Girl in the Park

Just the other day, I walked to the park
I had my earphones plugged into my ears
I was creating stories
There was a little girl there, on the swings
She flew through the air with glee
Her dad was with her
He pushed her through the air
They both watched as I approached
I wanted to sit on the bench, and create stories
'Stop,' the little girl giggled to her father as I sat
I heard her over the music
He held the swing and she swayed from side to side
She pulled herself off the swing
They both stood there and stared at me
They walked over to me
The little girl reached out. 'Play with me.'
I hesitated. I was yet to complete the scene in my head
It was my favourite part of the song
They were screaming of death and blood
'Come play,' she insisted
She had an ice-cream smile with dimples of dough
Her eyes were like mine
She is mine

Surrender

Give me the pills
I will drink them like wine
allow their brilliance
to dry my tears
my marriage medication
stitching me up tight
like good Greek girls

Give me the pills
bring forth the love
I want to smile
be the perfect wife
the mothering mother
I want to bury the beast
vanish into wog* myth
the one who lost the plot
but found her way back

luckily

Give me the pills
I want to dine and dance at weddings
be dazzled by the dress
push prams around the burbs

gather at mothers' group mumblings
have dinner parties
cuddle on the couch
shop your money
wherever

Give me the pills
so I can become
what is expected
and understood
so my parents approve
and my sisters love me

Give me the pills
so I can become
what everyone wants

Just give me the pills

She Takes Care of Me

In a room where sunshine peeps
and butterflies are doona warm
she takes care of me

breath lighter than clouds
my only oxygen, cushioning
nose to button nose, powdery skin
her small hand, brushes away
the hair, from my face
she traces my eyebrows
says they're her rainbows

you're Alice in wonder
but I'm not, I'm not
you are, Mummy, you are
you're Alice in wonder

in pitch-fork nights
she takes my hand
why you sad, Mummy?
Mummy just needs to cry
but why, Mummy, why?
You know when you cry
because you can't find your dolly?

Mummy just needs to find her dolly
Here, I cuddle you, Mummy, cuddle

when she's nowhere to be seen
and her toys whisper in hisses
when books are swallowed
then burned at the stake

don't *you* worry: *she* takes care of me

Out

I gotta get me out of this life
I gotta get me out
I'm not sure where I'll go
or what I'll take
all I know is I've gotta go

I won't pack much
a few jumpers, some jeans
enough to fill a backpack
I'll have to take credit cards
and my music
a notebook and pen

It's all I'll need for where I'm going

I know it'll be hard to go
I'm not sure if I'll ever come back
I won't tell them I'm going
I'll just have to sneak away in the night
They won't understand if I tell them I'm going
He'll try and stop me and she'll cry
Her little brain don't get liberation
It doesn't understand conventions
and norms, entrapment and isolation

It just understands Playschool
chocolate and play dough

So I won't tell them I'm going
I'll just have to sneak away

like a frightened woman in the night

Escape

Space

alone space alone space alone space alone space alone space alone
space alone need alone space alone space alone space alone space
alone space alone for   alone space alone space alone space alone
space alone space alone own   alone in   your space alone space
alone space alone space alone space alone space alone space alone
space alone space alone space me   to   alone space alone space
alone space alone space give   space alone find   alone space alone
space alone space alone space alone space alone the   alone space
alone space alone space alone space alone space alone space alone
space alone space alone space alone space alone space alone space

Cade Way

The houses are all relatively new in the
old Commonwealth games athletes' village
in Parkville opposite CSIRO
houses and apartments
now occupied by students and cute families,
boxed residencies, pristine lawns,
looks like you could almost
start all over again here

My friend rents a unit
in this village on Cade Way
It has really high ceilings
white on white suffocation,
this building was previously
a hospital for psychiatric patients
you can almost hear screams in the night
or maybe that's just me

She is also a writer, a bit all over the place
she bounces off one wall, I bounce off the other,
she isn't sure if I should be here
but the marriage counsellor suggested
some time apart from my husband
'breathing space' she called it
but when I go home to him I end up crying again,

can't stop crying at the dinner table
my little girl is confused
and I say 'Mummy will be okay,
Mummy and Daddy will figure this out'
but she just continues to stare at me
and I just keep on crying and crying
husband doesn't know what to do with me
both don't know what the hell is going on

and so I go back to Cade Way again
stop crying, make myself some pasta
we read our tarot cards and she freaks out
says she needs some space,
the old housemate is coming back
and I am not sure where I fit into the equation,
she's not sure if she wants to help me out anymore,
doesn't want to be the person who split up a family
barely sleep that night
she's not around when I get up
gone to school I suppose
not sure what to do with myself
doesn't come home that night either
and I worry because I am used to having
someone come home

wake up the next day
with a man on the living room floor

says he is the housemate
the lease is under his name
wants us both out
he seems friendly
but she isn't home
and I'm trying not to feel scared

I ring her when I leave that morning
she doesn't know what to do
we meet at her uni and search Gum Tree
she uses one computer, I use another
she is used to doing this
has done it many times before
doing her PhD, insanely smart
strict Italian background
nothing I'm a stranger to
been on the run since she could talk
tough enough to leave whereas I wasn't
I am learning survival tactics here
do my own searches on Gum Tree
didn't even know about Gum Tree before this point,
not sure what I am doing, adrenalin, finding, searching,
just don't want to go back home and cry anymore ...

The Mirror

she is weak weak weak weak weak weak *I* selfish selfish mother selfish selfish yes

shame you you bring shame to us you *you you* what do we tell people what do we

you idiot I hope you find what it is *you you you* are looking for in life idiot idiot

if you are going to act like an aussie* *you are special* we are going to treat you like one

sacrifice you are meant to sacrifice *you are beautiful* like we sacrificed sacrificed you

fuck you fuck you hi it's me me it's *you are worth more* beep beep beep fuck you loser

fuck you dickhead fuck you you *nobody else you you you* does that to me nobody rude

I will die if you do ena pethano* *you you are an artist you* ena pethano I will die I will

force force got to force got to *I love you love you love you* be be who they want me to

it would be easier so much *love you love you love you you* easier if if I was normal

normal normal normal really *you strong strong you are* want to be normal normal

can't won't won't can't love love *I love do you do love I do* again won't love again can't

die die die die hate hate you hate *you need to trust it* hate hate hate die die hate die

ugly ugly selfish mother selfish *trust yourself trust* shit mum shit shit shit useless

forever alone you will be alone die *it's going to be* alone alone you will end up alone

who would love you nobody will *okay it's all* nobody could love you nobody no

what has she she done she will never *going to be* happy crazy she is crazy lost the plot

words the poetry the book the music *okay* the art has driven her mad words words

you are dead to me I never want to see *you* again never never you are nothing to me

alone alone alone alone alone alone *I* alone alone alone alone alone alone alone

Living Alone

For the first time in my life, living alone
wasn't allowed to move out of home
before I got married
even though I wanted to
was scratching out
got married instead
and now look, what
I'm living alone, breathing alone
cooking alone, except when she's home
my pretty little princess
who didn't ask for this
my pretty little princess
who didn't ask for this
I am sleeping alone
when she's at her dad's
I am completely alone
forced to shut out my family
and their views on normal
they have no idea where I am
and neither do I, I never will
I wake in the middle of every night
crippled by the gaping space in my chest
strangulation, suffocation around my neck
I have nobody to turn to
other than the man

I am trying to get away from
I am living alone
inside the nightmare of my mind
can't get back to sleep
after the wake-in-fright
moment in the night
I search for comfort
in the dark corners
restlessness, breathlessness
I have no idea, I have no clue
where to turn, what to do
living alone, I am alone
this is alone, what I wanted
I am searching, I don't know
I wanted this, I am living this
Completely, and utterly, alone

Separation Steps

Mummy, when are you going to come home, when are you
    going to come home?
Number 57 tram, a little girl who looks like mine
Mummy, where are you, Mummy, where are you?
I'm at the new house, but we both still love you so much,
    baby
Mummy, what are you doing? You doing a poem?
Yeah, I'm doing a poem
Mummy, what are you doing? Mummy, what are you doing?
What are you doing, Mummy? What are you doing,
    Mummy?
WHAT ARE YOU DOING!
She's crying, refusing to nap, and I'm on the brink, I'm on
    the brink …
I want my daddy, I want my daddy, daddy …
Nightly phone call, punishment served
Mummy, I need you to come home
I can't, baby
I need you, Mummy
I can't
Please, Mummy, please
I can't
Please, Mummy, Mummy, Mummy
Shhhh …
Mummy

♫ Twinkle, twinkle little star

Mummy

♫ How I wonder what you are

Mummy

♫ Up above the world so high

♫ Like a diamond in the sky

♫ Twinkle, twinkle little star

♫ How I wonder what you are

Escape

All my life they've tried to control me
So I ran away. I ran away from the wogs*
I changed my phone number
I changed my address
Nobody knows where I live
Finally, I've escaped them
After all these years, I've done it

Now I live downstairs in a double-storey house
(it's completely self-contained)
There are chickens in the backyard
and a huge veggie garden and fruit trees
The furniture's not the best
(it's old and woggy but it'll do)
and the crochet blankets
smell like the ones at *Yiayia's** house
in the remote villages of Cyprus

The elderly couple upstairs are really nice
although the man stares into my window sometimes
but the woman brings me cakes when she bakes
(delicious, better than Mum's!)
She offered me dinner once but I declined
(need to keep that distance)

They also have a little table outside my door
where they leave me little presents
like broccoli from the garden and eggs
They go to church on Sundays
and just the other day the woman said
I should pray to God to help me

It's all good now with the wogs upstairs
But I think I'm going to have to move soon ...

When I Used to Write in Secret

When I was little I was shy and quiet
When I was little, I cried all the time & Dad said to me

you got to try, try not be weak

When I was seventeen I wanted to study art
When I was eighteen Dad said to study business
When I was eighteen I studied business
When I was nineteen my parents took me to a psychiatrist
When I was nineteen I had to be on pills or I would kill
    myself
When I was twenty-one I got a business job
When I was twenty-two I got married so I could move out
When I was twenty-five it was time to have a baby
When I was twenty-five I had to stop the pills to get
    pregnant
When I was twenty-five I was writing in secret
When I was twenty-five I dreamed of being a writer
When I was twenty-five, for one moment, I was brave
    enough
to tell one of my second cousins that I am writing

& she said to me

she said, *who's going to care what you have to say?*

So I pushed down the writing for two years

When I was twenty-seven, I gave birth to my daughter and
    my creativity
When I was twenty-seven I told my parents I was writing
When I was twenty-seven I was told I have responsibilities
When I was twenty-eight I was told I have responsibilities
When I was twenty-nine I was told to stop writing
When I was thirty I was told to stop writing
When I was thirty-one I fled my marriage and my culture
When I was thirty-one I had to shut my family out
because they wanted me to remain repressed and normal

And that's when I gave myself permission to write

Love According to Wogs*

Be who we want you to be
and we will love you
Fulfil your womanly duties
pop them out like popcorn
sacrifice like we sacrificed
and we will love you

we will love you, daughter
we will love you, sister
we will love you, cousin
we will love you

We are solid, like brick
not like the bloody *Afstrali**
we will overfill you with love
one oily dish at a time

In times of need we help each other
Even when we turn our back
withhold and trap
we are helping, you'll see
(it's the evil eye, she needs blessing)

Listen, we love you:
Honour thy husband

Respect your parents
Clean your house
Take your pills
Be normal and the rest
will love itself

The Centrelink* Queue

I'm in the Centrelink queue
I'm waiting in the Centrelink queue
I have fallen from wog* grace
and landed in the Centrelink queue
Got a two-hour car spot outside
I'll be lucky if I'm out of here in two hours
My feet are getting tired waiting in the Centrelink queue
I need to go to the bathroom
but I might lose my spot in the Centrelink queue
I'd probably take five years off Dad's life
if he saw me in the Centrelink queue,
add a few years to Mum's depression
Single separated mother in the Centrelink queue
Single separated mother in the Centrelink queue
Head low in the Centrelink queue
Loser in the Centrelink queue
The girl with the business degree in the Centrelink queue

I paid for the privilege of the Centrelink queue
when I worked for corporate giants
Forty cents in the dollar tax for the Centrelink queue
Forty cents in the dollar tax for the Centrelink queue
Not that that makes a difference in the Centrelink queue
I'm just a CRN number in the Centrelink queue
My arty friends are also in the Centrelink queue

The government financially supports us in the Centrelink
    queue
Artist funding in the Centrelink queue
Artist funding in the Centrelink queue
How this country supports arts, the Centrelink queue
How Melbourne has a vibrant culture, the Centrelink
    queue
The artist's shame, the Centrelink queue
Fallen from grace to the Centrelink queue
From the migrant dream to the Centrelink queue
I'm standing in the Centrelink queue

This is my shame, the Centrelink queue

The Dan on Saturdays

Every Saturday at 2pm
I go to the Dan O'Connell pub
with my notebook
and I write a poem
whilst listening to others read
on the open mic
and then I get up
and perform the poem
I have just written

I go to the Dan on Saturdays
because I have nowhere else to go
If my parents saw me in this pub
It'd be the biggest humiliation of their lives,
their degree-qualified daughter
hanging out with weirdo, Aussie* poets

I see you smiling at me after my poem
I don't know who you are but I think
you are an attractive woman
and already I know we are
going to be friends
'Hi, I'm Loretta,' you say
'Hi,' I say,

'I'm separated and I miss my baby'
'That's understandable,' you say,
'It must be hard, culturally.
You are one brave woman'

Yes. Brave

Wogs* are so afraid of being alone
they spend their whole lives clinging
But there is no such concept as alone
if you don't want there to be
All you have to do is want people

On the Red Carpet at The Tote

On the red carpet at The Tote, I sit cross-legged, stare up at my stars. In here, nobody can find me. In this dimly-lit space I am encased in a melody, safely spaced between a guitar riff and a voice, the bass line and drum thrash. This roof and these walls shield me from their stares.

The wog* stares.

Outside the sun is setting and through the windows there are people having a BBQ. There aren't many people here, but that's okay, it's our little secret: the best bands in Melbourne aren't on the radio, they play here.

Shh ... Shh ...

I'm not here alone. I'm here with my notebook.

On the red carpet at The Tote, I am safe.
Nobody can find me, they can't find me, see me for what I really am.

The music is loud, it vibrates through me, shakes her out, shakes out the tortured me, replaces her with the laughing, lighter me. Shake her out. Shake her out so I can be me again. Beat my wounded heart with your drum sticks, resuscitate me. Electrify my insides, kill the old, allow the new. Bring me forth and keep me.

On the red carpet of The Tote I am me, I am absolved, I am home.

I ran away from your face. I drove my restlessness to the nearest gig to drown myself in Melbourne's melodious melancholy.

I like this band. Eve's Protege. Great voice, deep, like Creed. It gravitates. Interesting mix of acoustic and electric guitar. Elements coming together, different parts, different creative parts, coming together, to create one piece of art.

One solitary sound.

Like with being with someone creative. I like how he plays guitar for me. It makes me think words. Intertwining our energies and then we're exploding and need space.

But I wouldn't want it any other way.

Moroccan Kings. I like this band too. Sarcastic, loopy. Their songs change direction halfway through. I like the unpredictability. And now he's screaming.

He's screaming her out.

Here I am safe. At The Tote I am safe. I am not part of
their bubble. I choose not to be. I choose to exist where I
choose to exist and I choose to sit on the red carpet at The
Tote.

When I Fucked for the First Time

It's like you never thought it would happen
but I needed to sever it

I didn't even like the guy

I told you on the phone I slept with him
& you shouted 'you fucking bitch'
& you shouted it again and again
& the whole street would have heard
you shouted louder than you had a right to
but loud enough so I got what I deserved

The Reading Glasses

They're lost, forever
a pair of eyes that magnified
misplaced in my own stupidity
in a dash for the train
or dropped rushing to school,
abandoned absentmindedly
grumbling at grocery shopping
stumbling somewhere
nowhere, not sure where

like my life

and not even Snow White knows
if she took them, played with them
hid them to punish me
instead she reminds me
in my almond-eye reflection
that Mummy can just buy new ones

I can just buy new ones

Every word I read pays a penalty
fogged headaches, disorientation

like the universe is trying to tell me
stealing the words from my veins

I imagine them on the ground
amongst grass, in the dark
their blue case, the specs
waiting patiently inside
for me to slip them on
the sparkling sides
my purple perception
I want to cry for them
cradle them like a lost friend
tears cried on shoulders
the life lessons

my mind criss-crosses over days
where I went, what I did
what went wrong
my memory blurring
like my vision
words we read together
stories shaped, lived
a life clarified …

and I just want to see again

The Apartment

It's no longer ours
our memories sold
to the highest bidder
my novice smile
your curing predictability
and now there is no
tangible asset
no proof we were once

happy

The Orthodox Baptism

I didn't want to go but knew I had to
So I put on my Sunday best, and went
Sealed in the car I played
Bullet for my Valentine
really loud

Everyone was really happy to see me
but I was a little overwhelmed
The double-sided kisses
the wog* embraces
the priest
I tried to smile
but mostly I was shaky

There was lots of dancing afterwards
(what us wogs do best)
but the food took a while
and the sweaty owner of the *taverna**
was running all over the place
and I was forgetting to breathe
between photos and conversations
while I contemplated leaving
but I couldn't leave without eating

I had to eat, I had to
because that's what us wogs do

and finally the food came
and I quickly scoffed it down
said the necessary goodbyes
ducking out before anyone
could stop me
around the corner
to a pub on Smith street
and once again sealed myself in
for some live Aussie* music
and a tall, long glass
of myself

Dead or Divorced

It's better to be dead than divorced
because then you can be mourned,
adorned, adored,
exactly the way
they wanted you to be

That's it, write me off,
and finally, we can live on the same page
Mother, father, sister and brother
The happiest of wog* families

You can dress me in your elegant eloquence
The daughter of your dreams,
and the rest can be a mere nightmare
one that can be woken from
with a strong, Greek cup of coffee

It's better to be dead than divorced
because then misery can be short-lived
and depression has an endpoint

You won't have to grieve the gossiping Greeks
Hide underneath your solid house of bricks

Shh, I won't tell if you won't

O Theos na tin anabafsi
May God rest her soul
Kali Orthodoxi kobela itane
She was a good Orthodox girl
Pige ke sto barebistimio
She went to university, got a business degree
Married in the Orthodox Church
Two well-behaved children
Ta kaimena
Poor things
A big house in the suburbs
Right on the river
E, O Theos na tin anabafsi
May God rest her soul

In an Instant

I closed my eyes
and five years went by

It's time for big girl world now
You even know how to pose for the camera
dressed in chequered school uniform,
ready to address numbers, shapes and people
I don't worry about you adjusting

You wheel a princess suitcase
from my place to your dad's
every few days,
wondrous, glorious, you
split between two worlds
I look at you sometimes and think:
How can something so beautiful
be mine

and his
in love with someone else now
I keep dreaming about him
and I'm not sure why
He says we'll always be best friends
but I have my doubts about that
and Disneyland

Mummy, are there princesses in our world?
No, they're pretend
Daddy said they're at Disneyland, are they, Mummy, are
   they?
Yeah, they're in Disneyland
Daddy said we'll all go one day, will we, Mummy, will we?
Maybe
I love you, Mummy
I love you from here to Disneyland
I love you from here to Disneyland times two!

Five years, in an instant
from curled baby toes to school dresses
from happily family to broken divorced
from shrouded in conservatism to exploding out of myself
I closed my eyes, and five years went by, in an instant

Yiayia Mou (My Grandmother)

It was my ex who told me you died, *Yiayia*
My family don't have my phone number,
they don't even know where I live
You're probably up there wondering why,
Yiayia mou, it's too complicated to explain
Don't worry your mind, rest, *Yiayia*, rest your tired mind

My ex rang to tell me you'd finally died, *Yiayia*
and the tears still linger in my eyes, refuse to trickle
I'm still suffering the effects of that drink last night
staying out late, partying with the Aussies*

I remember when the old me visited Cyprus six years ago,
    Yiayia
how you sat in your black, widow memory, stared at the
    walls
Your womb bore twelve children, two stillborn
and you've got so many grandchildren
you've lost their names

Every morning as we sat in the living room, you'd ask who
    I was
and I'd have to explain I'm your granddaughter
that we share the same name,
and you'd scan the room looking for Mum

just in case you'd somehow missed her walking through the
    front door
and I'd have to calm you, explain mum is back home, in
    Australia

When you asked if I like Australia and I said 'yes'
you seemed disappointed,
and I wanted so much to say, I love Cyprus better, but
    instead I just smiled
But then you clenched your fist hard, said that when I
    return to Australia
I must gather my family, my cousins, my aunties, my uncles
I must hire a big ship, you said, and return to Cyprus
return to you, where I belong

'All day and all night I sit here and wait,' she said,
'I sit here and cry for you all to come back.
How many days must I sit here and wait?
How many days?? How many days??'

I took her hand, reassured her panic, her impatience,
because tomorrow a fresh leaf would be turned in her
    mind
and this conversation, this moment, my image
would vanish into the unknown, just like we all did

She sat in silence for a while, twirling her thumbs, frowning
until finally she unlocked the treasure chest
the long ago memories of her mind
'I didn't want to marry your grandfather,' she said
'I was in love with another man.
But my brothers would not have it.
They dragged me by hair on Tuesday and on Wednesday
　　and Thursday
and on Saturday they forced me to the church and we
　　married
And when I sat beside your grandfather
I said "*this* is my fortune, *this* is my destiny",
and I accepted it, and I loved him'

Then an abrupt memory came to her:

'She didn't want to leave,' she cried
'She didn't want to leave!

"Keep me a little room, Mum
I don't need much, just a room
I don't want to go to foreign lands!
Don't worry about a dowry, Mum
I don't want to marry
I just need a room, Mum
Don't send me away, Mum,
Don't send me away!"

and on the day she left, the ship was sailing away
and I held onto that wire fence
and they were pulling me off
But I wouldn't let go
I couldn't let go!
I couldn't let go!'

Yiayia mou, don't let go, *Yiayia mou*, don't let go!

'That was the day,' she whispered to me
'That was the day, *agabi mou**
the day I lost my mind'

The Only Guarantees in Life

are there are no guarantees
Life owes you nothing
It does not guarantee life-long love
And even in the security of marriage
and all the kids you could conjure,
someone could die, and then what?
You could die—you could die tomorrow
You could sacrifice yourself for your kids
and they could end up hating you
You could sacrifice yourself for your partner
and they could end up cheating on you

You will not find happiness
in the heart of a plasma tv,
only toxic heavy metals
The dishwasher may make
your dishes sparkle,
and your oversized oven
may cook the best roasts,
but it's only food,
which we have to eat
to survive

If I could smash all the shiny stuff I would,
with the sledgehammer,

then I'd smash anyone else
who tried to get in my way
I'd live in a small room
with only the necessities,
and I'd ban anything shiny
I wouldn't buy a house
I'd live like a gypsy,
drifting from place to place
like music from a guitar riff
and I'd ride the melody
all the way to my soul
write the words
abandon control

Even with all the riches
of a thousand kings
Nobody owes you happiness
Nobody is responsible for it

only you are

only you

Soul Mate

We were sitting in the living room
lounging and laughing about
when it hit me,
and I wanted to
still it like a photograph

Our conversation is catchy confident
a developed understood understanding
When we're apart we're together
our touch, only a thought away

She climbs into bed when I'm asleep
her breath, squishy lolly sweet
I joke about buttering up her bot bot
baking it in the oven, eating it like muffins

Even when the clouds are gloomy grey
she tells me everything's going to be okay
and we run, hand in hand, in the rain
without an umbrella, towards the rainbow

Sure she steps out of line from time to time
demands that she wants everything
complains about my disinterest in footy
she reads the Target catalogue on the toilet

asks why I don't have a penis
and always puts floaties in my drink
She's hit me a few times
(she goes to the naughty corner for that)
but it's okay, in love things are never perfect
and I'm her first serious relationship

She's into all that girly stuff, which I'm so not
but somebody's got to wear the pants
She likes patting my face, arranging my hair
When I'm frocking up she marvels at my beauty,
showers me with admiration
I mean, what more could a girl want?
And no man would even come close
to looking at me like she does
For I've searched far and wide
in all places and spaces
only to find her,
the love of my life
born from my very
own womb

Me vs Moth

All my life I have been scared of moths
Afraid of them fluttering over my skin
pirouetting in my hair,
all while I'm unaware
eyes shut to the world

But the other night, I came home,
switched my bedroom light on
only to be greeted with the biggest moth
I have ever seen in my entire life

I was completely alone
It was just me, and the moth

It was about the size of a tennis ball
double the size of the moth my ex conquered
when we were married
and I thought that was the biggest moth
I had seen in my entire life

My initial instinct was to do what I usually do,
screech, run about the house like a girl
I had no fly spray
I had nothing but myself

But this time I didn't run
I froze, nailed my eyes on the fucker
I had never killed a moth without fly spray
I always got other people to kill them for me

Not this time

I armed myself with a few towels, shoes,
whatever I could find
I went over the plan in my head
the strategy to go in for the attack
retreat for the retaliation
then I armed myself
and began

I threw a towel and retreated,
repeated again and again
but it wouldn't die, no matter what I did
it kept fluttering around the light
prancing its existence, its fat, yellow body
its intrusive wings
and soon I ran out of towels, and shoes
so I had to go back in and retrieve more ammo
and I just kept throwing things
my aim was precise
a ninety-five percent hit rate
but still it would not die

and minutes went by, ten, fifteen, twenty
but I wouldn't falter, I couldn't falter
I was going to kill this fucker
I was going to show it
I was going to show this
Goddam mother of a world
that I was not going to be
defined by my fear

Finally, after an hour
it fell to the floor unexpectedly, mid-flight
taking me by surprise ...
I picked it up with a tissue
tossed it in the bin
DONE

When I Said I Still Loved Him

I didn't really have a choice
had to process it really fast,
that you were moving into
my old house with your children

It didn't seem to bother you
that I was still married to him
but I wanted to make it work
for the sake of my child

When I came over when my
princess was sick
while he was at work
(with your permission)
& I started to cry in my kitchen
& you hugged me &
said you understood
I, in fact, believed you

I said, *it's hard because*
I still love him
& you said
that you still love
the father of your children

& you can completely
understand

It was reassuring to receive
such comfort from you

I was so wrong

The Shock

The shock was when you said
it was now inappropriate that we be friends
It came like an earthquake
I was swallowed into

Gone were your promises to look after me
Gone was your commitment that what was
in the best interests of our daughter
was for us to be unified
& that you would never be
with a woman who didn't
understand that

You informed me of the new priorities
& suddenly everything changed

Our Ten Years of Papers

Suburbs away from the
middle-class dream I once lived,
I stumble into my flat, walls cracked,
cold and on my own
my floor covered in divorce disarray
don't know what to say to friends anymore
keep it piled inside,
got to cook dinner
then it's back to work
I have papers due to my lawyer
and this is turning into a full-time job

These are our ten years of papers, electronic and hard
I sift through dollar figures in your documents
from when you backed up our lives
on my external hard drive,
never realised while we were married
that your tendency to record all transactions,
every one of our life events
might be classed as an illness

Maybe you and I aren't so different after all

Thousands upon thousands of entries
divided into years, can search by category,

debits and credits to particular accounts
the creation of all these documents
just in case you ever needed it

It seems that the time has arrived

I search for who contributed what in the beginning
no matter how much I look, I can't find it
You were so good at saying so much
never really good at stating the obvious

The lawyers want me to produce more papers
take notes every day on what happens
between us and our daughter
I think I've hit page thirty-three
This could turn into a novel
You always encouraged my writing
Now I'm writing our story
You and your bullshit promises
We've been separated two years
And this is still going
Writing more papers
Drowning in our ten years of papers
More and more coming
And I wonder when I will
See light again ...

Sticky Single Mum Stigma

Sticky single mum stigma sticks to my white pages, sticks to my trembling hands, write, write with sticky single mum ink, stick, stick, stick to the path, stick, stick, sticky single mum stigma all over my body, draws me down, down, down, sticky single mum stigma in my heart, open too wide, the room fills, stills, walk away from sticky single mum responsibility, sticky, sticky, sticky, sticky, sticky single mum love, don't get too close it's sticky, lost, lost, lost in sticky single mum flood, sticky single mum insanity, catch, catch, catch a thick breath in the sticky single mum ocean, waves, waves of sticky single mum judgment, sticks to silly little school shoes, hold my hand, my princess, sticks, stick, don't look, sliding sticky single mum tears, walk, walk, stick to sticky single mum cement, push, push, walk, push, push, stickier, harder, push, stickier, sticky single mum how can you do all this, sticky single mum, you have everything, sticky single mum, we will push you over because we can, sticky single mum, who do you think you are doing all that you do, sticky, sticky, sticky, let's make it stickier for you, stay locked away, sticky single mum, but go back to work, sticky single mum, just don't achieve anything, don't achieve more than we can, sticky single mum, stick, stick, stay stuck in your stereotype, sticky single mum, don't fight it, don't try, stay there, stay stuck, sticky single mum, stick there, stay there unloved, so we can feel better about ourselves sticky single mum, stick, stick, stick ...

Life

It never turns out like you planned,
or maybe it does, but you're not prepared
Yet somehow I feel cheated
out of the Greek myth I was raised in,
the perfect picket fence

It was chainsawed to woodchips
I scramble for the pieces
to puzzle us back together
when I don't really want to
Your house, our old sanctuary
Your new joy, my cemetery
You've already renovated me out
added a new coat of paint to the fence
and suddenly, I don't live anywhere

I say this to my mum
as I lay on her couch
and she takes care of me
because I can barely move,
the alleged ulcer in my stomach
expanding every time I think

You're dying inside me
burning my lining

I cough up the acid
of what has happened
the remnants of us

they pumped me with the drugs
at the hospital yesterday

yes, fill me with drugs
pump the fence to oblivion

when the doctor came to my house
and told me to go to the hospital
it was the middle of the night
and I was alone
like I will be from now on

I watch the hospital chair
my dad sitting in your place
you call and say you want to visit
but I don't want you to
tied together forever by our daughter
I squeeze the blanket
petrified by my body's protest
the doctors still aren't sure
what is going on and I repeat
It's over, It's over, It's over ...

Me and My Naked Body

I never liked looking at my body in the mirror
and now, it's kind of a betrayal
this year, the year overruled by my body,
ulcers burning my insides, compounding pain
endometriosis and God knows what else
flowering in my womanly parts
spreading like weeds
to other organs

My lover once ripped off my clothes
because I couldn't stand the sight of
skin stretched, sin bulging and exposed

quickly, cover me up, quickly …

The other day my daughter
wanted to get changed at the pools in front of everyone,
and she wouldn't listen, she couldn't understand
why we had to get changed in the change rooms,
we have to get changed in the change rooms,
please, listen—would you just listen!

I don't want people to see your vagina! LISTEN!

Innocence glistening away …

I'm looking in the mirror
skinnier than I usually would be,
undies and singlet, my legs, no, my legs ...
And not that I would ever look at myself naked, no, no, no
    way ...

When I was little
I accidentally saw Dad showering
He was furious at Mum

Dirty, disgusting, pleasure is wrong dirty, don't touch
yourself, shouldn't touch yourself, I am going to chop your
fingers off the next time I catch you, you should pray to God to
forgive you, Mum, please don't tell Dad, he'll hit me, no sex
till you're married, look at the walls! Dirty TV shows! Look
at the walls! Look at the walls! You have to be a virgin, be a
virgin, no boyfriends, no sex, sex is wrong, sex is right with
your husband, but sex is wrong, sex is bad, I can't have sex,
it hurts, can't fuck my own husband, what is wrong with me,
pain, you want me, come and get me, your sex, our sex, sweet,
bitter pain, pain, pain, bad, bad, bad ...

When they operate on me soon
they should stick a shovel in and
scoop out all the womanly parts
that seem to control me
They should de-sex me

so I can never think sex
dream sex, want sex,
they should de-pleasure me

My body. Are you denying or inspiring me?
Maybe I should play some music to eradicate all this
Something nice like 'The Summer' by Josh Pyke
It's on a CD that my friend gave me
and it reminds me
of laying in the park with her
and the sun on our bodies

Now there is a new man in my life
'Let's take our clothes off,' he said to me yesterday
My body shook its head. Nothing against you, but no
He kissed my forehead. He held me

My body, one day you and I
we *will* love each other
We will look into a mirror
me and my naked body
and we won't be two entities
divided by pain and the past
One day, we *will*
love each other
In the meantime
let's go to bed
and rest

Home to Heal

You can't run away from yourself forever
no matter how many men you marry
You can dance your way from club to club
but you'll just end up at the start
Lips to lips searching for the perfect kiss
A sexual encounter of complete bliss
But the universe always has a way
of bringing you back to the start

Ten years is a mere blink
and it's back to the beginning
under Mum and Dad's roof,
carrying in my stomach
the stinging ulcer of the past
and some other health issues
requiring further testing
(but I know what's really going on)

I've come home to heal

Because I like laying on their couch
and watching *Modern Family*
or having my sister
flick my destructive lover
from her knee

like he's a flea
and be protective over me

or telling Dad I'm going to watch *Sex and the City* on tv
and Dad pretending like it's no big deal, crossing his legs
ten years of 'walls' and bad habits forced down
by him liking having me around
he endures us in the same room
while Samantha is fucking her latest fling

Because after arguing the same issues
over and over and over again
divorce, disappointment and all the rest
people just plateau and start loving you,
and it's nice being nurtured and cared for
and learning not to speak
when one regresses
into tiresome habits

And it's amazing how much more
willing a person can be
to make another person
a Greek coffee
when they are asked nicely,
and respectfully
After thirty-two years,
I think they are starting to see

I'm not conservative
After thirty-two years
I think I'm starting to see
that they aren't so bad
They just did the best they could
And that my family are pretty cool

I think we are really starting to like each other

And I don't actually want to go
back to my place and be lonely
In fact, I am enjoying
digging a hole in this house
planting my flag
staking my claim
THIS IS WHO I AM
I am your daughter
and I require your love
Yes, please take care of me
because it's never too late
I've been through a lot
these last few years
and I am tired
so please help

Backyard Flood

I have wanted the heavens to open all my life
And open they did, thirty-two years later
Christmas Day at Mum and Dad's
Hail the size of lemons from our tree
Sheltered from the havoc we knew was due
We all stood on the back veranda
Watched in amazement the desecration
The fruit on the trees hang defeated, pierced by bullets
The wog* veggie garden they spent their life
Tilling and sowing, it is drowning
The gutters are overflowing
Dad goes inside in a panic
The ceiling is leaking
They all run in
But I stay still
The air is fresh
Finally, I can *feel*
It's kind of nice, this storm
The hail calming to light rain
Backyard flood
It's over now
Dirt foundations washed away
Wog drama going on inside
But we are all still standing

It's kind of nice this storm
The clouds are shifting
And I anticipate the sun, soon

Burn

After the court case is over
Our two year legal battle
I'm going to get in my car
With all my abdominal cramping
Then I am going to drive to the bank
Tell the teller to withdraw all of my settlement
The money I was always entitled to
But that you and your commander
Wanted to pound me into the ground for
Because you operate under the preconceived, sexist notion
That mothers de-skilling at home to look after *your* kids
While fathers climb the corporate ladder
Is 'equal team work' not 'piggy back riding'
I'm going to withdraw it
The thousands and thousands of dollars
Count the crisp bills one by one
Pile them neatly in a box
Then I am going to drive to your house
Lay the box on your doorstep

Light a match
Throw it in

Watch our life burn
Flames in my eyes

Inhale the fresh smoke
I'll ring your doorbell
Get in my car
Drive away

The Price of Happiness

What is the price of happiness?
I have paid dearly for mine
like a loan from the bank of life
indebted, I pay, I pay, I pay,
sneak sleep between seconds,
be the breadwinner, the mother,
the protector, the inspirer

How much does happiness cost?
Two years of legal fees and counting
Two stomach ulcers
Womanly parts entangled in endo
Two heartbroken parents
One disillusioned sister
One confused child
and counting

But I'm okay, I'm okay
I don't want people to worry, I'm tough
I just dread the day my body says
enough is enough

Happier but harder, I tell people
when they ask if I regret it
I'm happier but it's harder

See, my back pain hurts more
Sometimes it throbs to the rhythm of
'you should have stayed' because then
I wouldn't have to worry about money
have a beautiful house in the suburbs
be able to relax, and my child would be okay

And I was looking at my hands the other day
The lines have doubled deeper
And my hair was so much thicker

I'm so tired I'm operating with my eyes asleep
I stay up late when I know I should have gone to bed when
    she did
Because at 3:30pm tomorrow when I'm driving to pick her
    up from school
I'll be feeling it, prying my eyes open

What is the price of happiness?

I'm still mourning *Sleeping Beauty*
That's what I'm doing after she's gone to bed
I'm mourning *Sleeping Beauty*

Married for almost ten years! At twenty-two!
How did I get here?
The price of happiness

To be able to lay on the couch
without laptop keys tapping in the other room
Just to lay on my couch in peace, and breathe

And I can't even contemplate a relationship,
of trusting someone enough
to allow them into my fortified reality
only to have it crumble again

How do I trust again?
He is already married
And I still can't trust

Then I meet you
But you are buried so deep in your pain
You are unreachable
And I no longer own the excavation tools to find you
Not the breath to revive you
And so, from time to time
When our paths cross
We hug
And it's nice

This is my life, all mine

Happier but harder, I tell people
Happier but harder

All Care, No Responsibility

The aqua-blue hospital curtains hang in air-conditioned
    hum
embroidered, leaf-shaped bubbles falling
Day four in the short-stay ward
stressful self-inflicted sickness
womanly parts have once again waged war

The PA calls out lotto combinations:
MET Call Fourth Floor Room Twenty-seven Bed One
MET Call Fourth Floor Room Twenty-seven Bed One
MET Call Fourth Floor Room Twenty-seven Bed One

Lucky me not dying, in a private room
precious blue, orangey-fire sunset view all of my own
Thank you, Mother Earth, for allowing me
to grace your valleys, drink from your streams
bathe in your brilliance, write and describe the journey

Woman across the way gets wheeled out by paramedics
leaves behind the silent shudder 'lymph nodes'
nurse blanket-tucks her in with 'all the best, darl, all the
    best'
hand sanitises in preparation for the next patient

'All care no responsibility,' the Greek nurse said in
    emergency
in response to my trying to make sense of his profession
attempting to pierce my skin for a drip
eyes harder than both our failed, long wog* marriages
hands soft enough to touch our broken children

The other nurse couldn't get it in
blood trickling down my arm, bypassed my heart
'Gee you've got hard veins,' he mumbled to himself
rather than to my stubborn hand,
but don't I know it, don't I fucking know it
blinking white on impending-court-case white custody
    battle
it hasn't been long, cubicle two, nice to see you again

I don't care about the mess, as long as I get a vein
I don't care about the mess ...

Xipna, ti ehis? Xipna * speaking to me in Greek
'It's in, wake up, take some deep breaths
talk to me about what you write,' holding my hand
'How do you do this job? People dying around you ... '
wanted me to look him in the eyes but couldn't, wouldn't
insisted, was adamant, *kita me sta matia,* look me in the
    eyes:

'Because I like caring for people but when I go home
you're not coming home with me
After my shift I'll sit on my back veranda
with my *tsigaro** and my *kafedaki**
and I'll forget all about you.'

'All care, no responsibility,' he said

Sounds like someone I know

'That's why you can never be a paramedic,' he said
'And that's why you can never be a poet,' I replied
'Exactly,' we said

Five days later, I start writing the poem

You'll Eventually Stop Crying

You feel like dying
but you'll eventually stop crying
when the whirling windstorm dissipates
and you can finally see your eyes
for the first time

You're tired of fighting, can't keep trying
everything's hard, tainted with fright
just cry, let it be, it's better to give in
accept the challenge of what life is
It's not a sign of weakness,
but rather acceptance, wisdom
you've learnt your limitations
know your capabilities

Min valis do nou sou me dous belous, Mum says
'Don't equate your common-sense with one who cannot
    see reason'
You might feel like you're walking away with nothing
but trust me, you are walking away with something
much more valuable that money will never be able to buy

Nothing seems to be going right in your life
trust me, it won't be long until you're alright
You know you've felt this way before

that the feelings have eventually fluttered out the door
Take stock of the certains in your life
Bring them close to your chest
Hold on really tight
Accept this is where you are at
You'll eventually stop crying
It's going to be alright
You'll eventually stop crying
You will

shh woman

The Woman

It's not about trying to be the woman
It's about just *being* the woman

Be Her

It's about seeing the woman
You can see her
She's right in front of you
You can touch her
There she is

I thought it was about *trying*
working hard for years
Reaching for her
Striving to become her

But I always fell short

Then someone told me
all the cells in our body
regenerate
and your body
is an entire new body
every seven years

A new me

So I made a list:
I wanted her to be organised
I wanted her to sleep well at night
to not allow stressful thoughts
to occupy her strong mind
I wanted her to be calm
to not allow situations and people
to get the better of her
I wanted her to have self-confidence
be proud of who she is
I wanted her to be wise
forgiving, intelligent,
a capable mother
a loving daughter
a loyal friend
a fun sister
a great person
that smiles & is happy
& is kind to herself

I wanted her to have the ability
to force anxiety out of her body
And keep it out

I thought about how she would act
What she would say
How she would carry herself

An image began to form

I could see her
Touch her

So I made a decision

To become her
To be disciplined to *be* her
To *stay* her

I took a step forward

And I became her

I am her

The woman

Missing in Brunswick

When I woke up this morning
I turned on my phone in bed,
was greeted with an sms:

I am serious, my sister said
You are not going to be catching the tram again at night
A girl went missing in Brunswick

I googled 'girl missing in Brunswick'
and couldn't believe how gorgeous she was,
scrummaged for evidence
amongst mass media spin
that she was a drug addict or something,
didn't find anything except smooth, glowing skin
bright ABC presenter eyes,
couldn't get out of bed for a while,
lay there and listened to the innocence
of Brunswick birds chirping

I love living in Brunswick
because it's Barkley Square wog deli
mixed in with Retreat punk bands,
because the streets are narrow,
houses bunched up like wog* families,

almost like Cyprus safety,
you can call out to your neighbours
from across the street,
mine are elderly Greek,
look out for me
because I'm a single mum
always on the run

When a girl got assaulted
just off my street months ago
I told the elderly man
who reminds me of my dad
that I was really, really worried

No, nothing will happen here
You are safe, they just wanted her money
Don't worry, min ta skeftese afta ta pragmata
Don't worry about these things

I too walk home in the dark, Jill,
just a couple of minutes
a quick dash from the tram stop
look over shoulder once, twice, again
quick breath, cross the road randomly
and you always think
there'll be enough time to scream

I've dabbled at Sydney Road bars
Brunswick Green, Bar Etiquette
and you just extinguish that niggle
at the corner of your mind, like you probably did
when your friend offered to walk you home
and you said 'no, no, no, I'm just down the road'
because we're independent women
and we're not going to let fear
ruin our lives, or else,
what's the point in living here?

They found your handbag in a laneway just off Hope Street,
graffiti walls, heritage, cobblestone floors
Your senses dampened with one too many drinks,
he would have been quick, dragged you right in
before you knew who was what
and now you're gone like magic,
and it's as if you never walked down Hope Street

Or maybe a weirdo guy saw you at The Green,
was staring at you but you took no note of him,
weirdos always look at you because you're stunning,
and he was probably thinking
I'm gonna follow this chick
because this is my lucky day
This, This, *This* was his lucky
fucking lucky *fucking* lucky **fucking** day

You rang your brother on the way home
It was 1:45 am but he was in Perth,
said you sounded worried
Maybe you already knew
someone was following you
but didn't want to worry anyone
You look like the kind of girl
that wouldn't want to worry anyone
I do that too sometimes
when it's dark and I'm walking,
call someone on the phone
so you have backup
in case someone grabs you

Your husband rang your mobile
from 2am to 6am non-stop
He went looking for you at 4am
At 6am your mobile went straight
to message bank,
probably ran out of battery,
the last strand of energy
before it surrendered and died

27,360 likes on Facebook and counting
Office Works glossy coloured posters
plastered on poles along Sydney Road
They locked off Hope Street to look for you

But you were wearing almost all black
Black clothes to match your black curls
A stunning image of woman
You went missing on Hope Street
Missing on Hope Street
Jill, you went missing on Hope Street

Anxiety

It all started with an idea, a new year's resolution
to confront situations in person rather than in writing
A poetry colleague, after seeing my show,
enquired if I am able to confront situations
with the same bravery I have on stage

At the time I laughed it off, said I couldn't possibly
It was the reason why I performed
I can't deal with things in reality

I didn't tell her I had a fear of people yelling at me,
like they could somehow turn into my dad from
twenty years ago

I sat and reflected on this idea, for recently I observed,
that it wasn't confrontation that caused the anxiety,
it was any kind of situation where I could possibly
end up disappointed, even small, work-related stuff

It was then that I realised how much anxiety has always
dominated and controlled my life,
at every turn, every meeting or email,
it was there, affecting the outcome

'You should channel that anxiety,' my poetry colleague said,
'like you do on stage. If you could do that,
you would be a force to be reckoned with'

So I set myself up a meeting where I would confront
a very powerful man: my divorce lawyer
There I would explain how they had deceived me
and how I wanted all my money back

When I got there, I pretended I was getting ready to go on
    stage
It was exactly the same feeling, the anxiety rising from my
    gut
But just like when I am going to perform
I didn't allow it to get to my mind and cloud it
because that's when you lose your lines
It's all about regulation, knowing you are the one in control
Nobody can get you when you are up on stage
But nobody has the right to do that in life either

He did raise his voice but so did I
'Why don't we get out the document
where you glamorised my case?' I said

You knew I would lose
You kept the case going

I lost so much of my life savings
You played on my vulnerability
You came to see my show!
My ex has an infinite pool of my money
You knew I never stood a chance

I sent a rocket through my lawyers that day
Afterwards Dad said, 'you di no le
him get one word in. You wer tough!'

I didn't get the money back, but I rest my case

If I Were a Man

If I were a man
I would sit with my legs spread
hands behind my head
and I'd totally get the world
to go down on me

The world is a cocksucker, bitch
I'd moan and I'd groan
& I'd watch its red lips sucking my cock
& I'd be like *yeah, fucking suck that cock*

I'd operate my affairs like this
Divorce lawyer, accountant or artist
It wouldn't really matter what I was
I'd cum in every single one
of those bitches' mouths,
relish in my wallet's and my ego's
gradual & eventual erection

I'd be king of the fucking world

The men I respect, they'll get
a collaborative handshake
& the women I respect

will get that all-alluring charm
that makes the world go
round and round &
up and down
on my cock

If I were a man, I'd totally objectify women
Have them feeling not thin enough, not pretty enough
I'd have them eating out of my hand
I'd flirt and I'd work it
I'd tell them what they want to hear,
be kind and suggestive,
get in and have a little play with their heart

I'd be an equal opportunity employer
Equal all the way down to my cock
Women get less, but they'll get more
if they undress, act aloof,
don't challenge my integrity,
nod and be the good girls they're meant to be,
then they'll get equal pay and benefits
But equal to a certain point
because the world is a cunt not a cock
Don't get me wrong! I'd love women!
But we can't have female emotions
running the show

If I were a man
I'd totally work it baby
Let them think
it's their work I respect
when it's really their mouth
that I want enclosed around my cock
I'd do what it takes to make things go my way,
you just got to know what buttons to push
to open the door to their woman
Tell them what they want to hear
Give them a hug, a smile
Let them know you are really truly there for them
By the time they realise what's what
You've shafted them
Fucked them in the cunt,
up the arse, in their heart
and assumed your throne
at the top of the world

If I were a man
Oh, if I were a man!
If I were a man
I would sit with my legs spread
hands behind my head
and I'd totally get the world
to go down on me

& I'd cum in its mouth
again and again and again

Oh, If I were a man

Swallow

When you've swallowed thirty years of silence,
words sometimes come out
angry

I Want to Rip off My Vagina

I want to rip off my vagina
I want to knead down my breasts
until my chest is buff
and muscly

Just like a black man
may at moments
want to immerse himself
in a bath of white

out of anger, or frustration,
acceptance or surrender
that the world is as it is

Just like this

I no longer want to be female

I want to cut out my emotions
replace them with bricks

I want a dick
I don't want nice nails
I can paint pink

I want to rip off my vagina
with hot wax

& then I want to go for a long run

I want to run and run and run

with my balls dangling between my legs

I want to walk down my street
at 2am in the morning
& not be afraid
I will get raped

I want to be physically strong
I want to be powerful
I don't want to be vulnerable
I want my daughter to feel
just as safe with me
as she does with her dad

I want to be a white, middle-class male!

I want to be able to write anything
that I want to write and
still be respected
the same way a male

would be if he wrote it

I don't want people to take advantage of me

I want a female to wait on me
and dote on me
and cook for me
and I want to feel okay about it
because that's the way
the world works

I don't want to be judged as hysterical
when I speak up about being
treated unfairly

There is nothing I want more

Rip it off, tear it off
Get me out
I'm screaming out
I am shrilling out
Get me out of this body
Get me out! Get me out!
Rip off my vagina
Tear out my womb

I want to be a man

To the Orthodox Greek School at the Church

Thanks for taking on my daughter, I really appreciate it
It's good for the new generation to learn some Greek,
to pass it on into the future
I am proud of being able to speak Greek,
proud of my Greek-Cypriot roots—
Heaven Forbid the culture die out
down here in the Great Oz

It's a bit of an inconvenience,
having to drop her off to class each week
(being a single mum)
but I'm coping, I'm OK
I would have preferred to take her to a Greek school
that wasn't religious, but Mum and Dad insisted
'cause apparently it's the right thing to do
& maybe somehow they think I'll become religious again
God love 'em, my parents, I really, really do,
they try so hard, but they don't understand
how much it grates on me when my little one
insists on wearing a cross every day
because she thinks that's the only way
her and I will be reunited when we're dead
It's like that little cross is carrying the hurt of my past,
weighing down on her tiny little neck

See, I would have preferred to take her to a Greek school
that wasn't religious, but money's a bit tight this year
& these days the church will take anyone they can,
just to keep the tradition going,
and the faith going and the fear going,
and the priest said I can bring my daughter for free, you see,
for the first year, but it's been three years now,
and although money is a bit better,
I can't justify handing over
my hard earned single mum dollars to you,
Greek Orthodox priest at the local church
I try to, but I can't do it

Maybe we should consider it ... compensation,
for all the hurt and the fear and the pain
the Greek Orthodox Church injected into me,
why don't we consider it compensation,
for the Greek Orthodox Church youth group
my parents sent me to went I was sixteen,
as a way to help me with my sadness,
let's consider it *compensation*
for the countless times you scared the life out of me,
strangled me with your rules and your confession
and your heaven and hell and purity and sin
to the point where I couldn't look myself in the mirror
to the point where I despised my own self-image,

how it scarred me so deep that all I saw was blood
and communion and judgment,
and all life became for me was an enemy
I wanted to eradicate, or burn
in the depths of hell,
me and my pain
for all of eternity

Don't worry about me now, Greek priest at the local
    church,
I'm totally fine. The day I gave up on your teachings and
    God,
the day I realised that being a good person had nothing to
    do
with believing in anything, the day I threw everything out
    the window
and started to believe in myself, I got better
I'm heaps stronger, thanks for asking
Maybe one day we'll be able to sit in the same room and talk
But I've got a long way to go before I get there,
& I suppose you have too

In the meantime, I'll take my

Compensation

Shh, Woman, Shh

Woman, why're you so loud?
You're too chatty
too whiny, too observant
You should shh a little, shh

Everyone in the cinema can hear you
Your laughter is louder than all the rest
You never used to laugh like that
six years ago when you were
married & repressed
You sound really, really happy
But the entire cinema wants to
lean over and tap you on the shoulder

to say *Shh*

You won't get anywhere in life
You won't get a man talking like that

writing like that
being like that

Take a leaf out of your past and shh
Remember how you always shushed?

Do more of that, be more womanly,
more motherly, more elegant

Smile for the camera, shh
Swallow your laughter, shh
Be polite, shh, shh, shh

Employers want to hire women
who are part of the all-male team
so don't speak inappropriately
don't challenge
don't question
don't dream
everything will come good for you
you'll have everything you want
and everything you need
trust me on this
the only way to succeed
is to bring your lips together

&

Shh

That's it

Shh, shh, shh

What I Learned from the Handmaid's Tale

The thing is, I'm just really sad since watching it
I know it's only a TV show, a story, but it's not, not really
I don't know what to say other than I feel feverishly shit
My only comfort to huddle like the handmaids do
Together with all the women in the world so we can cry in
    chorus
Even though we don't trust each other
Compete in whispers to trample through the funnel for air
I started watching the series *The Handmaid's Tale* at 10pm
    one night
I was conscious of the time and school drop off in the
    morning
Being a single mum, can't afford too many late nights
But as soon as I saw Offred and her forced foetal offering
Her world controlled by Gilead's Christian fundamentalists
(not ISIS, that's Islamic fundamentalists which is different)
Her screams swallowed and gagged on until nothing came
    out
I couldn't move, my gaze super-glued to her plight
And I couldn't leave her alone trapped inside the TV
To be fucked between the Father and the Mother and the
    Holy Fucking Spirit

So I made the decision to stay up all night until I saved her

In the morning I woke exhausted having had little sleep
and failed my mission

I told myself it was just a story by my favourite writer and
poet, Margaret Atwood

I hadn't read the book yet, and I was cursing myself that I
should have by now

Margaret wrote her story in the 80s

But is it really a story or a terrifying premonition?

Sometimes fiction is just a stone's throw away from fact

Or maybe a rendition of something we pretend isn't
happening

Thirty years later it seems the same issues are lingering

Except feminism and capitalism have morphed into some
deformed monster

Or maybe that has always been the case

Margaret's tale had me thinking back to my first poetry
class

How I asked my teacher about rules and she told me there
are none

I didn't consider her a feminist as she was old and grey

But I guess she was because she showed me pages of
writing by feminists

It was Margaret's and Sylvia's and Patti's poetry that
resurrected me

Their words had me questioning the cultural, sexual and
religious repression

I had inherited like a birthright spawned from patriarchy
Never had I considered I had choices
I married when I was only a baby
So in poetry class I took to the notebook with bound
hands
Wrote till blood soaked my clothes and I was considered
mad
Sex poetry came out of me until I was labelled a slut
I like to be fucked, so to men and the literati I made sense
I fought so hard to be free even my tears became blood
Wiped with the tissues of women I had never met wanting
to be my friend
But I didn't realise till I watched the last episode of *The
Handmaid's Tale*
Which was years after my emancipation
That my hands are still bound
Bashed, shoved, murdered, controlled, fucked in every way
possible
I still exist under the foot of a man
The palace of patriarchy still reigns
Did anyone actually ever ask us
If we actually want to fulfil our biological destinies
Under His fucking Eye?
Margaret's metaphor opens us up to consider
Gilead could happen even today
All that's needed is some crazy man

With sexist, religious, racist beliefs
Who has access to chemical warfare and bombs
To execute a Handmaid's order
And suddenly Gilead is just a stone's throw away from now
However, what I learned from *The Handmaid's Tale*
Apart from how fucked the world was for Margaret
That she resorted to write such a disturbing and
    traumatising tale
Is how fucked the world still is today
But despite this, even in the most repressive circumstances
Where speaking up is punishable by death
The controlling power will push forbidden and wicked
    ways underground
But human nature is to fight even silently, to rise
And I learned that the resilience of women
The gender that bears the world in her womb then births it
Bleeds her dirty sin though her uterus and out of her
    vagina
Will find a slow, but gradual way, to an almost freedom
I also learned that Canada is the best country in the world
Even in the land of fiction, in the past and in the now
Especially when it comes to treating refugees
And every other country is pretty shit
It probably came as a shock of course
When white people were watching *The Handmaid's Tale*
That the refugees were westerners (unlike today)

So they were probably relieved when Canada handed them
A phone card, money, clothes, food etc
Rather than a big fuck off and go back to where you came
    from
I don't know how Margaret came up with this story
But it had me crying like a scared child
Longing to slash my wrists in the bathtub

What It's Like Having an Ex-Husband

Who is this man who stands before me
with the deceptive friendly eyes?
How can it be that your seed gave me life?
I defend our child and you yell like you used to,
back in the days when I thought fighting was a normal
yet uncomfortable duty every relationship bore,
our only model our parents,
it was only when I became undrugged
under your recommendation we conceive,
that the veil slowly began to lift,
being dragged through years of your
childhood trauma & anger,
I have paid dearly for the wisdom of
how cleverly charm can deceive

Every time I find a way to do good
your woman undermines it,
hidden behind your weakness,
your obsession with nuclear family,
you deliver her barks viscerally,
yank olive branch after olive branch
from my hand and burn them
I know you know it's bad for our child
that we don't get along,

but it's like you don't care, you just don't care
you'd happily dance on my grave given the opportunity

My opinion comes last in your new ways
Pile your pride high with dollar bills
& mansions to feed your woman's wills
You rely on the fact that
I will comfort our daughter's shrills in the night

When does divorce pain die?
It's like it plagues inside you
Twist my words to justify your decision
with an abundance of money you've bought the law
our circumstance is a metaphor
for everything that's wrong with the world

Oh—my curse for being female
I was born to be destroyed
When will womanhood be free?
How resilient the woman can be!
Everyone was on your side when we broke up
(because you never bashed me)
Everyone always points at the woman

When your ego somehow convinces you
that you still have the right to yell at me,

I break down & need to talk to my friends
I cry so much, like all the pain
that's connected to the divorce—
my marriage, why I got married, my family pain,
my parents, their pain, the migrant experience—
it gets woken from a deep death slumber,
it gets triggered by this event,
I cry out the entire history of my pain,
and then, my emotions hit a wall
& I snap back to being okay,
to stagnant, to reality, my daughter,
and the wound scars over and sleeps,
lays dormant until the next time you pick

& this process, I see it in our daughter,
every time she is overwhelmed by your regime,
dividing her life down to her undies and socks,
she cries up all of her short past,
all the inflicted wounds,
I put her to bed rambling about
why we are not together anymore
even though it's been years
and she wakes up in the morning
like nothing happened

Life didn't have to be this way for us,
we could have been friends like we planned,

kept the communication open for our daughter,
but it's too bad, your dick had other plans

It's hard getting all this down
I've wanted to get this stuff out for years
I don't want my daughter to read all this
how it is between us
all you've done
how you financially ruined me
because hurting the mum is hurting the child
& you've made me so sick
you've actually affected my health
this never-ending divorce has aged me
but if I don't get all this stuff down
if I don't get it out
I won't function tomorrow,
and I need to be there for our daughter
so either way I lose

And I know this poem is too long,
And it's probably not in the best poetic structure,
but it was poetry that has spared me
a life with you, poem by poem,
it pulled me out of the canyon of our relationship
and here I am today, still climbing,
still fighting your existence,

your presence in my life, one poem at a time,
until one day, I am finally, free of you

Line in the sand

Photograph at a Poetry Gig

I find two photos on my computer
from a while back
emailed to me by a photographer

One is of me reading my poetry
and I am sad looking down at my paper
like I am not sure
I deserve the space

But little as you are
you have your arm high
protective around my waist
you stare out at the crowd
like you *get it*
clutching our children's book
a funny little story
about how you sniffed up a bug
we wrote it together
you illustrated it
we created a dream
it would be a series about you and me

The second photo is a little more relaxed
me, seated on the stage
reading the stapled children's book

you standing behind me
too shy to read
your hand on my shoulder
you giggle, so proud
deliriously happy
as I read out our story
didn't realise you were
my biggest supporter
long before I could ever be

Line in the Sand

On my birthday the moon is eclipsing,
the first I've witnessed in my existence

We stand in the dark
& look up

It doesn't look like it's moving

& young as she is she says

Sometimes things move slowly
But they are still moving, Mummy

After I tuck her into slumber
I ponder, I cry & then

I draw a line in the sand

then I turn around
& stare at my reflection:

you're not sure how to begin
where to step forward
but you know you must step

can't stay like this anymore

so I start with
you can't undo the past

embrace all your actions
the good and the bad

take accountability and responsibility

stop taking it upon yourself
to make others do the same

each to their own

step away & turn away &
walk away
from pain

un-attach

down to the local fish and chip shop

say *hello how are you!* on arrival
& hope you have a great day!
as you're leaving with your food
It feels nice

Especially when they respond with

You too, love!

& think, it might be really nice
to spend some time
with good old you
for a change

For example: who are you?

give yourself a cuddle

go on!

cuddle you!

& have a nice, restful sleep

The Pleasing Woman

If you spend your life trying to please others
for fear of losing their love,
you will always fall short of pleasing yourself
and you will never love yourself
the way you were meant to ...

Believe

Lately, a few new people
have come into my life
who believe in me

There seems to be a lot of

belief in me

Even my mum recently
stuck up for me
when someone took a dig
at why I do my art instead
of work fulltime
and she said, she said
you will do your art
& you no need to
explain dis to nobody!

I've spent many years trying to get people to support me
& now that they are, and things are coming good
something still isn't quite right
because it seems that despite the people
who rally around me
who try to catch me just as I'm falling

I still seem to be failing and repeating
the same pattern over and over again

& that's when I realised

there's one person
one pivotal person
who doesn't believe in me
who stops me from achieving
everything I dream for

& that person is

ME

Because if you don't believe in yourself
you will keep failing and falling and tripping
& you may as well stop trying all together

Because if you don't believe in yourself
if you don't believe in who you are
if you don't believe you can have the love
& the career and everything you dream of

it won't happen

and you leave yourself open,
vulnerable to the next person who comes by
who doesn't believe in you at all,
that person will knock you down
and they will take pleasure in it
& the disappointments will pile high to the ceiling
& all you will do is sit and look at them all day
and beat yourself up about who you are
and you will fall & get up, fall and get up,
and you will spend the rest of your life
doing this again and again and again

But if you stand solid and strong,
if you stand tall behind the path
you have chosen for your life,
the decisions you have made—
If you stand tall inside *you*
& say this is who I am
I am awesome
I believe in me
I believe I am a
good, honest and
decent person
with great intentions

If you believe

You are one step closer
to achieving what you want

But if you don't believe
you may as well stop trying
because you will always
get in the way

of you

A Different Way

Don't be afraid to try out
      A different way of doing things
It's not success or failure
Look at it as an experiment
Practising until you get it
                just right

Onto Happiness Now

Enough pain
Onto happiness now
Onto joy, now
Onto my daughter's smile
Enough of hard relationships now
Onto good connections now
Onto love from friends
and love from family
Enough of tears now
onto smiles now
onto moving away from bad now
no more bad now
just good now
onto happiness now
happiness now
happy now
happy

You Survive

When people or situations
or life get you down
& it's like you're laying
ten feet underground
Remember
you've been here before
you've broken out
You survived

This Is My Voice

This is my voice
This *is* my voice
This is *my* voice

I have spent so many years repulsed by
the words coming out of my mouth,
like they're poison, venom—wrong
But this is my voice
No need to be ashamed
This is my voice

Glossary

Broadmeadows: A working class suburb of the northern suburbs of Melbourne

Wog: In Australian English wog was originally a pejorative for Mediterranean migrants, though in recent decades its offensiveness has been defused in certain contexts by common usage in pop-culture produced by the descendants of Mediterranean migrants.

Tihous: Greek word for 'walls'. Often shouted at children of migrants when sexual activity was depicted on television so they would look away.

Ta Rialia: The title of a song by Michalis Violaris who popularised music sung in the Cypriot dialect when *Ta Rialia* was in the top-ten charts of Greece in 1973.

Syrto: a Greek folk dance.

Ena bethano: I will die (Cypriot dialect).

Aussie: Short for Australian but the term is typically used by a migrant or a person descending from migrants as a label for a person born in Australia descending from Anglo-Saxons.

Yiayia: grandmother

Afstrali: Australians

Centrelink: The Australian government's welfare system.

Taverna: tavern

Agabi mou: my love

Xipna, ti ehis? Xipna: wake up, what's wrong? Wake up.

Tsigaro: cigarette

Kafedaki: Greek coffee

Credits

'All the Effort', published in Czech in *Partonyma,* issues 35-36, volume 9, 2020, University of Pardubice.

'Dead or Divorced', published in Polish and English in *Fragile* magazine (Poland), issue 4(46), 2019.

'I Can't Wait to Take You to Crèche Tomorrow', published in *Social Alternatives* (Volume 31 No.2) by University of the Sunshine Coast, 2012.

'Love According to Wogs', published in *Offset* (No. 12) by Victoria University, 2012. Film produced by Outside The Box Press, 2013.

'On the Red Carpet at The Tote', published in *Etchings: Three Chords & the Truth* by Ilura Press, 2013.

'Orthodox God', published in *Southern Sun, Aegean Light: Poetry of Second-Generation Greek-Australians* by Australian Scholarly Publishing, 2011.

'Missing in Brunswick', longlisted for the FISH Prize (Ireland), 2013. This poem is part one of three parts.

'Motherhood Observations', published in *Page 17*, 2010.

'Shh, Woman, shh', was turned into a film in 2019 in Poland. It was translated into Czech and published in *Partonyma,* issues 35-36, volume 9, 2020, University of Pardubice and in *In Your Bedroom, Your Cats Are Sleeping: Anthology of the literary quarterly Partonyma.* A selection from the years 2012-2021, 2021, University of Pardubice.

'Shopping' published in *Unusual Work* (No.18) by Collective Effort Press, 2015. Published in Czech in *Partonyma,* issues 35-36, volume 9, 2020, University of Pardubice.

'Space' published in *Unusual Work* (No.18) by Collective Effort Press, 2015.

'Surrender', published (English and Greek translation) in *Poetry in Dialogue* by Ideogramma, 2014. Published in Polish and English in *Fragile* magazine (Poland), issue 4(46), 2019. Shortlisted for the Doris Ledbetter Poetry Cup, 2010.

'Swallow', published in Polish and English in *Fragile* magazine (Poland), issue 4(46), 2019.

'The Apartment', published in *Sotto* by Australian Poetry, 2013.

'The Prayer of Blood', published in Polish and English in *Fragile* magazine (Poland), issue 4(46), 2019.

'This Is My Voice', published in Czech in *Partonyma,* issues 35-36, volume 9, 2020, University of Pardubice.

'What I Learned from the Handmaid's Tale', published in *Tuck Magazine*, 2018.

'Yiayia Mou' (My Grandmother), was turned into a film in 2022 in Cyprus.

—

Some of the poems in this book form the basis of Koraly Dimitriadis's poetic monologue, KORALY: "I say the wrong things all the time".

Acknowledgements

Thank you to Les Zigomanis, Maurice McNamara and David Cameron for their editorial support. To Sabina Hopfer and Christopher Lappas for layout and design and for being my publishing family. To Ania Walwicz for her open-minded, liberating poetic teachings and to all the other teachers who taught me in my professional writing and editing diploma at RMIT. To the Melbourne spoken word community who witnessed my emancipation and encouraged me and supported me through it all—and still do. To Christos Tsiolkas, for believing in my voice, never judging me and being a constant support. To Amy Bodossian for her friendship, long discussions, inspiration, hope, and for just being Amy Bodossian. To all the people who have sent me inspiring messages, or published any of my work, or supported any of my work, or anyone who just believes in my work and reads it or comes to my shows — thank you so much, it really motivates me to keep going.

And lastly but more importantly, thank you to my family for their eternal love and support. Thanks, babe, you know who you are. And to my wonderful, amazing daughter. Looking into your eyes is what I live for. I do it all for you.

About the Author

Koraly Dimitriadis is a Cypriot-Australian writer and performer. She has had poems published in Polish, Czech, Greek and Greek-Cypriot, and her short stories, essays and poems have been published in *Southerly, Etchings, Overland, Unusual Works, Social Alternatives, Meanjin, Solid Air* (UQP), *Resilience* (Ultimo/Mascara), *Foyer* (UK) and others.

Koraly's poetry films have been shortlisted for prizes, screened at festivals and have been televised. Koraly has performed internationally, including at The Poetry Café (London) and The Bowery (New York). Koraly's poetic theatre monologue "I say the wrong things all the time" premiered at La Mama. Koraly performed in Outer Urban Projects's Poetic License (Melbourne Writers Festival, 45 Downstairs, Darebin Arts).

Koraly's essays/opinion articles have been published widely across Australia, including international publications *The Independent* (UK), *Shondaland, The Guardian, The Washington Post* and *Al Jazeera*. Koraly is a professional member of the American Society of Journalists and Authors.

For her fiction manuscript, *We Never Said Goodbye*, Koraly was awarded residencies at UNESCO City of Literature (Krakow), Wheeler Centre, Chantilly, HOANI (Cyprus) and Moreland Council.

Koraly holds a diploma in professional writing/editing (RMIT) and a double degree in accounting/computing (Monash). She has spoken on panels, run workshops, taught poetry at RMIT, and has been interviewed on television and radio including ABC's "The Conversation Hour with Jon Faine".

www.koralydimitriadis.com

Index

CPSIA information can be obtained
at www.ICGtesting.com
Printed in the USA
BVHW052301100323
660193BV00010B/116